INTRODUCTION TO
FIRE OVER YORK

THIRTY odd years ago when Leo Kessler (aka Charles Whiting) published his first edition of this book (*The Great York Air Raid*), he gave the **Yorkshire Evening Press** and the **Yorkshire Post** the following account, somewhat tongue in cheek, of his own experience as a 15 year old teenager in the 'Great York Blitz':

"For me, of course, it had all been a bit of a lark. After nearly three years of waiting, when they finally came that early Wednesday morning in April 1942, dropping their "Christmas tree" flares across the centre of the old city, it meant excitement, the start of a big adventure for an impressionable fifteen-year-old. Almost as soon as the sirens started, there were significant thuds all around and through the bedroom window I could see the unnatural glare of magnesium from the incendiaries burning on the roofs opposite. **This was it!**

My father, in his Home Guard uniform, was already in control, shepherding the neighbours inside the house (no one trusted the outside shelters – garden sheds with the window bricked up and an extra layer of concrete on the roof). Hurriedly, the women were shoved underneath the big kitchen table, while the men – my father, the neighbourhood warden (who had abandoned his post very smartish as soon as the first high explosive bomb dropped nearby) and I – stood guard. We'd all heard tales of Jerry parachutists being dropped during air raids.

In the event no **Fallschirmjäger** *came winging down. Instead, the hot water boiler in the corner burst, spraying the ample bottom of the lady from next door with scalding water. "I've been hit," she shrieked, "I'm bleeding!" at the same instant as the kitchen door blew off.*

My father was propelled by the rush of hot air from the kitchen into the next room, while soot came pouring down the chimney. The air raid warden began to blub and the fat lady's cries continued: "Won't anybody help me? I'm bleeding to death!" It was like a scene from an Ealing comedy. Later, after the Jerries had gone, I went outside to pick up shrapnel and spent bullets as souvenirs. I did not know till afterwards that 300 people had been killed or wounded that night and that one third of all homes had been damaged or destroyed. It was only later that I heard from a fellow fifth-former how he had watched our dead maths teacher being carried out of his wrecked flat on a door; from another, how he'd seen a delayed-action land mine explode the following morning and shower debris on a mother running with her pram. The little boy inside had been killed outright. But

---

for me, however, that German Baedeker raid on the fourth English cathedral city to be attacked would remain, as I grew up, something of a comic adventure. A bit of a lark.

Three years later, as an eighteen-year-old soldier in an armoured column working its way through Cologne in pursuit of the retreating Germans, I realised that I had been an innocent eye-witness, in part, to a dreadful and permanent change in the nature of air warfare".

Now three decades later, it gives me the greatest of pleasure to introduce a new third edition of one of Charles Whiting's favourite books (he has written over 300 and still at it) to a new public in Yorkshire and the world for that matter. Whether young or old, reading it for the first time or just refreshing your own experience during those fateful years, as we celebrate the 60th anniversary of VE Day, we will remember them.

Gillian Tidmus-Whiting
May 2005

Printed and published by

G.H.Smith
& Son
T H E   P R I N T E R S

The Advertiser Office, Market Place, Easingwold, York YO61 3AB
Tel. 01347 821329.   Fax 01347 822576.   ISDN 01347 821072
Email: info@ghsmith.com   Web: www.ghsmith.com

ISBN No. 0 904775 48 8
© July 2005 Charles Whiting

ONE: The Reason Why

'Terror can only be broken by terror. Everything else is nonsense. The British will only be halted when their own cities are destroyed. I can only win this war by dealing out more destruction to the enemy than he does to us!'

Adolf Hitler to Major Christian of the Luftwaffe, 1943

THE war came to Yorkshire on the afternoon of August 15th, 1940. On that warm Thursday afternoon, the little Wolds market town of Driffield was going about its business as usual. The two hotels, *The Bell* and *The Keys* were packed with Wolds farmers attending the corn market and off-duty airmen from the 77th and 102nd Squadrons, who flew out-of-date Whitely bombers from the airfield two miles up the road at Kellythorpe.

But as the farmers in their unseasonal tweeds drank ale and talked prices and the aircrew 'shot lines' about 'wizard prangs' and those who had already 'gone for a Burton', the war was on its way to Driffield. For, at 12.30 pm exactly, 50 'Junkers 88' bombers had crossed the Yorkshire coast and were now gaining height ready for the dive-bombing attack to come.

In *The Bell*, one farmer cocked his head to one side, mug poised at his mouth and said as he heard the sudden whine of aircraft engines, 'The RAF must have stepped up its training programme. There's a lot of planes up there.'

'Not bloody likely!' an RAF pilot explained. 'Those are Jerries!' He bolted for the door, followed by the rest of his crew. Teenager Thomas Overfield who saw the Germans coming into the attack still remembers 'that impressive formation as they lined up for the attack' . . . and 'the whine of those powerful engines as they brought the war to this quiet corner of England.'

Heslington Hall, Headquarters of No. 4 Bomber Group, which directed many of the RAF's bombing attacks on Northern Germany, such as those against Lübeck and Rostock.

And then it started. The RAF squadrons were caught completely by surprise. Aircraft after aircraft was destroyed. One hangar blew up. Another three were set on fire. Within minutes the whole airfield was a shambles of blazing hangars and wrecked aircraft. But in the midst of that chaotic disaster there was one happy man. A few weeks before, on a sudden impulse, the ground crew man had stepped into the cockpit of a Fairey Battle and had somehow managed to fly the plane all the way to a southern airfield where he had successfully landed it, although he had never flown a plane in his life before. The RAF had not been amused and he had been hurried off into the cells. Now the guardroom at Driffield fell apart all around him and he stepped out happily – a free man once more. For a little while.

In 1939, both sides had been content with dropping leaflets on each other.

By the time the raid was over and he was recaptured, Driffield Field had lost 12 bombers on the ground, four hangars had been destroyed, and the Field was out of action until the end of 1940. The war had come to Yorkshire at last.

Now as 1941 gave way to 1942, Yorkshire, and in particular its coast, remained virtually the only place in the country still subject to German air attacks. After Driffield, it was Bradford's turn. The raid was not very severe, but it did motivate the wool town's most famous son, novelist J. B. Priestley, to liken his home town to 'a giant super-human meat and potato pie with a magnificent brown crisp, artfully wrinkled succulent-looking crust . . . steaming away like mad. Every

"Here's Betty's Bar"

Betty's Bar, well-known 'hangout' for wartime aircrew.
Its fame spread so far that it featured in this Tatler cartoon of November 1944.

puff and jet of steam defied Hitler, Goering and the whole gang of them. It was glorious!'

What it all meant could have been anyone's guess, but it was all very folksy and Yorkshire stuff.

Leeds followed. Again the raid wasn't very severe. The Town Hall and the City Museum were badly damaged and several people had very unpleasant experiences, including one girl student on duty at the University's switchboard who, instead of waking up another girl needed in an emergency, alerted the august Vice-Chancellor – *at four o'clock on a cold winter's morning!*

* * *

Sheffield's treatment had been much, much harsher. Prior to the war, Professor Haldane had warned in his book *ARP*: 'There is half a square mile of Sheffield which is more vital to the production of munitions than any other part of Britain'. The Germans knew that too. Now they attempted to knock out this hub of the British armament industry.

Decoy lights out on the moors had helped to head off the raiders for a while and the first German bombs to fall had exploded harmlessly on Leash Fen outside the city. Now the bombers came in for the kill – some said, by following the tramlines glittering in the moonlight. Steelworker Mr. F. Barrows was just watching a 'corny gangster movie' in the Palace Cinema where the gangland boss, Edward Arnold, snarls to Robert Montgomery, *Shut that door!'*, when the first stick dropped. 'All the doors blew open – and the cinema emptied like magic!' he recorded, with a twinkle in his eyes, 40-odd years later. Soon the whole city centre was ablaze, with the fire services fighting desperately but unsuccessfully against the firestorm. In the end, 8,000 premises were destroyed in Sheffield and 85,000 damaged; 668 citizens were killed and 1,590 seriously injured. Something had to be done.

As the bombing of Yorkshire continued, the German attack now being concentrated on long suffering Hull, a new man took over the command of RAF Bomber Command. Once back in 1940 he had stood on the roof of the Air Ministry watching burning London and sworn that the Germans would reap a bitter harvest from the deadly seed they had sown over the British capital. Now Air Marshal Arthur 'Bert' Harris was in a position to carry out that threat.

Between 1939 and 1945 a total of 40 airfields spread across the county like a great aircraft carrier anchored off the coast of Europe. From these fields the young aircrews set off bravely each night for Germany.
Many of them ended up dead in some foreign field.

Lübeck's famed Holsten Tower, before the attack which led to the German reprisals, the 'Baedeker Raids'.

Harris, brisk, bluff, and abrasive, had come up the hard way. Off to Africa at the age of 16 with five pounds in his pocket, he had sought his fortune in farming, gold-mining, and driving horse teams. In 1914 he had joined the Rhodesia Regiment and fought German guerrillas, marching up and down East Africa for months on end until he had sworn he would never march again.

As soon as that campaign had ended, the browned-off infantryman had joined the Royal Flying Corps. During the interwar years he had slowly progressed up the ladder of promotion in the RAF, proving to be a very forceful character until eventually in early 1942 he had landed the plum job of chief of Bomber Command.

'There are a lot of people who say that bombing cannot win the war,' he declared a few weeks after taking up the appointment. 'My reply to that is that it has never been tried. *We shall see!*' Now in the early spring of 1942, Harris, decided that if he were to succeed, his first task was to find an easy target, both to locate and to bomb.

Fog dispersion for take-off

Dead British Flyer

He found it in the old German city of Lübeck. The port-city presented few problems to locate. It was situated on the Baltic coast and his bombers could fly over the undefended sea to attack it. It was lightly defended and was not incorporated in any of the powerful 'flak alleys', such as those of the Ruhr and the Southern German industrial cities. Above all, the city centre was made up of medieval, half-timbered houses, which were highly flammable. As Harris put it in his typical forthright manner: 'Lübeck was built more like a fire-lighter than a human habitation'. And he made no bones about his reason for selecting the target: 'I wanted my crews to be well-blooded, as they say in fox-hunting, *to have a taste of success for a change'*.

Lübeck: the Cathedral receives a direct hit, April 1942.

As 'Bomber' Harris intensified his campaign, scenes like this became commonplace in German cities. A woman views the damage in Hamburg, July '43.

Thus it was that on the night of March 28/29th, 1942, the RAF bombers began to take off on the first raid under 'Bomber' Harris's command. The crews which flew them – and it must be remembered that 56,000 of them would be dead before the war was over – came not only from Great Britain, but from half-a-dozen Commonwealth countries, too. Rhodesia, New Zealand, Australia, Canada, South Africa . . . they were all represented. There was even the 'R.T.A.F.' involved; otherwise known as the 'Royal Texan Air Force': Americans from Texas who had volunteered to fly for the Royal Canadian Air Force. In the mixed crews flying from Pocklington, only a dozen miles from Driffield where the air war had first struck Yorkshire, there were at least two Americans, who were temporary 'limeys' – Sergeant Charles Honeychurch from Brooklyn and Flight-Sergeant R. Campbell from Pawling, New York.

All of them had long been melted into one great unified force by mission after mission over the Reich; the pleasures of York's 'Betty's Bar' and 'The Half Moon'; the riotous mess parties where they bellowed out the chorus of *'Do You Know the Muffin Man?'*, as one by one they had tiptoed across the mess floor with pints of beer on their foreheads; and frenzied games of 'Flare-path', diving across the floor between two lines of human beacons clutching flaming newspapers. Doomed, brave young men, fated to die an early death.

But this night they were in luck. Out of the 300 bombers that had zoomed across the North Sea to strike Lübeck, only eight were shot down. The Hansa seaport was caught completely by surprise just as Harris had hoped. They started fires that took *32 hours* to put out, destroying 1,000 dwellings and damaging a further 4,000. Five hundred-odd innocent civilians were killed and a further 785 were wounded. Harris's strategy had been proved right, but the 'butchers bill' was terribly high.

British Tanks entering Münster, the terribly damaged Westphalian city, March 1945. Today happily and totally rebuilt Münster is York's twin city.

Next day, the German Minister of Propaganda, Dr Goebbels, known on account of his small stature and vitriolic tongue as the 'Poison Dwarf', wrote in his diary: 'This Sunday has been thoroughly spoiled by an exceptionally heavy air raid by the RAF on Lübeck. In the morning I received a very alarming report from our propaganda office there, which I first assumed to be exaggerated. In the course of the evening, however, I was informed of the seriousness of the situation by a long distance call from Kaufmann [Nazi *Gauleiter* of nearby Hamburg]. He believes that no German city has ever before been attacked so severely from the air. Conditions in parts of Lübeck are chaotic.'

Four days later the 'Poison Dwarf' wrote once more: 'The damage is really enormous. I have been shown a newsreel of the destruction [in Lübeck]. It is horrible. One can well imagine how such an awful bombing affects the population. Thank God, it is a North German population, which, on the whole, is much tougher than the Germans in the south... Nevertheless, we can't get away from the fact that the English air raids have increased in scope and importance.

Martin Bormann, Hitler's secretary, (above left) was a great advocate of unrestricted air warfare.

If they can be continued for weeks on these lines, they might, conceivably, have a demoralising effect on the population.'

Adolf Hitler was furious. He had always sworn that 'when the British Air Force drops two or three kilograms of bombs, then we will in one night drop 150 . . . 250 . . . 300 or 400 *thousand* kilograms! When they declare that they will increase their attacks on our cities, then we *will raze their cities to the ground!*' Now the British had bombed the ancient city of Lübeck with impunity.

When a few nights later the RAF bombed Rostock, also on the Baltic and of equally small military value, his rage knew no bounds. Although the *Luftwaffe* bomber fleet was fully committed in Russia, Hitler ordered that something must be done. *But what?*

By now most of Britain's major cities were well-protected by General Pile's anti-aircraft gunners and the increasingly effective British night fighters. The quality of the German bomber pilots still engaged in operations in the west had deteriorated alarmingly. They no longer pressed home their attacks with the same determination and courage as their predecessors had done back in 1940. How could pilots of this calibre be expected to penetrate the defences of London and Liverpool? Even Hull was becoming too much for them, although it was 'a soft option', which could be attacked from the sea.

General Milch, an implacable enemy of Britain, thought he had the answer. In the same month that Lübeck was so disastrously bombed, he started to make his plans to hit back. A new phase in the air war over Britain was about to begin.

It all started very inauspiciously.

One afternoon in early April, 1942, four Messerschmitt fighter-bombers dropped out of the sky off Torquay, that home of maiden ladies and retired gentlemen, and came racing in at 150 feet, their machine guns chattering. Almost before the genteel folk who lived at the seaside resort knew what was happening the Messerschmitts had dropped their bombs and were hurtling eastwards once more, back to France. It was reported that more than one lap-dog never got over the shock.

At top level no one took any notice of the raid. Torquay had no military value whatsoever. A few ladies might be in shock and in due course some irate gentleman would write to *The Times* protesting about the lack of defence at this 'delightful watering place'; that would be about the sum of it.

Four days later another puzzling target was attacked, Brixham. A week later Bognor Regis followed. Then it was Swanage's turn. Five days later Portland was attacked.

These 'tip-and-run' raids, as they were now being called, puzzled the British authorities. What was Jerry up to? For his part, General Pile of AA Command was inclined to find the raids, 'annoying but at the same time . . . a bit pointless'.

By the third week in April, Exmouth, Bexhill, Folkestone, Hastings, Lydd, Dungeness, Poling, Cowes and Newhaven had all been struck by these 'tip-and-run' raids; the phrase the popular press had coined. For the German fighter-bombers did not seem really to 'hit' a target but simply to 'tip' it. All were targets, too, of virtually no military importance; all were raided lightly and all were attacked during daylight hours.

Suddenly the raiders struck *at night* for the first time in a year. General Pile began to have his suspicions. He guessed the Germans were going to recommence night bombing. *But where?* His gunners effectively protected all major cities. Would he be justified in taking away some of his anti-aircraft batteries from these cities to defend what had been up to now regarded as 'open towns', places such as Guildford, Maidstone . . . York? Pile hesitated. He simply couldn't defend everything.

* * *

Hamburg at peace again

This new strategy had gained headlines in the German press and appeased the public, who were alarmed by the two devastating raids on Lübeck and Rostock. Now the Germans took it a stage further. The 'tip-and-run' raids had confused the British. It was time to make full use of that confusion.

On the night of April 24th, 1942, the Germans made a short sharp raid with 25 planes on the venerable cathedral city of Exeter. The defences there were non-existent; and the *Luftwaffe* deliberately set as their target the Cathedral and its surrounding area. They swamped that section of the city with incendiaries and heavy calibre bombs of a type never used before. The result was severe damage to the historic city. The choir aisle of the Cathedral was hit, both St. James's Chapel and the Sacristy were demolished; and most of the Cathedral's priceless medieval glass went too. Pile had been caught completely off guard and one of Britain's most important historic cities had been badly hurt.

Next morning *Radio Berlin* announced that, as a reprisal for the bombing of Lübeck and Rostock, 'we shall go all-out to bomb every building in Britain marked with three stars in the Baedeker Guide' (named after the famous German guidebook writer of the 19th century).

The 'Baedeker Raids' had commenced.

TWO: York, Anno'42

'Everyone who has no form of shelter should busy himself at once with selecting and preparing a refuge room'.

Ministry of Home Security leaflet, Sept. 1940.

T HE autumn when it had all started, you could buy 'fish and taties' at Lawson's fish shop in Penleys Grove Street for three-pence. A Ford 'Eight' bought off the peg in Piccadilly would have cost £115; and a plot of land for a 'semi' in Heworth would have set you back £60.

York in the autumn of 1939 had been a nice, cosy little world, with Messrs Terry's and Rowntrees doing good business, especially the latter with their newly introduced and very popular *Kit Kat* and *Black Magic* lines. Of course, there were still unemployed about. Young men in cloth caps and 'art silk' mufflers, furtively playing 'pitch and toss' for half-pennies in the back streets of the Groves and down the alleys running off Walmgate. But everyone agreed the new Conscription would soon take them into the rapidly expanding Army.

Admittedly, after the war scare of 1938, which had led to the Munich Conference, there had been some changes. ARP drills had been carried out on the Knavesmire. Gas masks had been hurriedly issued (cases supplied overnight by Rowntrees). Corporation dustcarts (horsedrawn still) had delivered makeshift lanterns to most street corners to be used in case of a blackout. But that was about it. York was still a sleepy provincial backwater where nothing exciting had happened since the Siege of 1644.

©www.petersmith.com
(Tel: 0870 2201 249)

York: the city as the German bomb-aimers would see it. In 1942, apart from a few bombs and many scares, the ancient city had remained virtually untouched. But the harrowing scenes witnessed in the bombed German cities would be seen here too.

Home Guard Called Out

To Help Police and Rescue Services

EVER since the Blitz on London it had been realised that the Home Guard could be called on to give substantial help to police and rescue services in the many incidents which resulted from an enemy attack. They were involved in rescue work, roping off areas with unexploded bombs, guarding approaches to danger areas, mounting guard on damaged property, diverting traffic and evacuating the civil population from damaged and unsafe districts.

Many of York's Home Guards rallied to the assistance of the Civil Defence Servies that night. The story is told of one group who 'arrested' a strange body of airmen who appeared in the city. Guarded by volunteers with fixed bayonets they were taken to headquarters where they were questioned. It could well have been a 'Dad's Army' scenario.

'Your name?'

'Alberto Perrugiano'

'Yours?'

'Silas P. Brown.' (In deep Hollywood accents)

The identity documents did not entirely confirm their statements and so the telephone wires hummed. Eventually from an airfield some miles away came the necessary confirmation. Who were these strange men? They were members of the American Eagle Squadron who had ventured into the city sightseeing earlier in the evening.

'You're darned cute and darned smart,' was the only comment they made when released.

All that had changed on that Sunday morning when it was announced by the BBC at 10 o'clock that the Prime Minister would speak to the nation at 11.15 am. Everyone knew why. Three days before, on September 1st, 1939, Germany had invaded Poland and so far there had been no reply from Hitler to the Premier's demand, made two days ago, that he should withdraw from that country.

Now they waited expectantly, listening to selections from *Princess Ida* and a recorded talk on *Making the Most of Tinned Food* until, finally, that tired old man, with his weary, sad voice, came on the air.

..Shoot straight, Lady

You've got a fighting job on hand, too. These are significant days and anyone — man, woman, or child — who is less than fighting fit is a pull back on the total war effort.

FOOD *is your munition of war.* The Government sees that you get the right stuff and it's vital that you should know how to use it to full advantage . . .

There's cheese : it makes muscle and bone.

There are potatoes : they give energy and warmth.

Carrots, that give vitality and help you to see in the dark.

Green vegetables, with their valuable salts and vitamins, which are so very important for clear complexions and sound teeth.

Did you know that 5 quarts of summer milk — milk at its richest and when it is most plentiful — go to the making of 1 lb. cheese ?

Or that swedes, the juice of which you used to give to babies because of its valuable Vitamin C, are now to be had at most greengrocers cheap enough and in big enough quantities for you to serve as a second or third vegetable to the entire family ?

All good live stuff. And you need them all : *every day.* Serve everything appetisingly as you so well can do. Then you can be proud of your vital, active part in the drive to Victory.

'I am speaking to you,' he told them, 'from the Cabinet Room at No 10 Downing Street. This morning the British ambassador in Berlin handed the German government a final note, stating that unless the British government heard from them by 11 o'clock that they were prepared at once to withdraw their troops from Poland, a state of war would exist between us. I have to tell you now that no such undertaking has been received, and that, consequently, this country is at war with Germany.'

The old man's voiced seemed to break slightly before he went on in his weary manner, 'May God bless you all! May He defend the right, for it is evil things that we shall be fighting against – brute force, bad faith, injustice, oppression and persecution; and against them I am certain that the right will prevail.' After over two decades of peace, Britain was at war with Germany once again.

Suddenly – startlingly – York was roused from its three centuries of sleep. Ration books were issued. Those who had the money to do so set off a run on the food shops. Little boys were organised to go from shop to shop to purchase tinned meats, corned beef, sugar, fats, anything that could be hoarded for the lean times to come. Reservists were called up. The Cavalry Barracks ran out of space. Hastily, church halls and the like were mobilised to take in the incoming soldiers. At places, such as the Methodist Hall in Brook Place, the Groves, the hapless reservists were locked in, as if they might well desert at the first opportunity. In order to obtain their precious 'fags', they were forced to toss threepenny bits over the high wall (it's still there) to the waiting youngsters who would run to fetch them *Woodbines* and *Park Drives* in return for the cigarette cards they contained.

A POW camp was opened on the Knavesmire. Some of its first denizens were German socialists and Jews, soon to be sent to the Isle of Man. Trenches were dug in the moat of the Bar Walls. The recruiting office, next to the Convent in Blossom Street, was flooded with volunteers; there were far too many of them for the harassed recruiting sergeants to deal with. All was hectic, exciting activity. For everyone knew that time was running out. At any moment the Germans might launch the same *blitzkrieg* against the west, as they had just unleashed on poor, hard-pressed Poland. Soon the sinister black Panzers might be rumbling across France towards the Channel. How long would it be before those fearsome Stukas with their hideous sirens began falling out of the skies above York to release their deadly little eggs? *'It won't be long now!'* they cried to one another that autumn, as they bustled about their new duties in the ARP and fire-watching services, as if they were privy to *Herr* Hitler's (for the BBC still addressed him so formally) innermost secrets.

* * *

Nothing happened! The *blitzkrieg* did not take place. Instead in the west there ensued the 'phoney war', where the first French casualty, unfortunately, was a deaf French farmhand shot by an over-zealous British sentry of the British Expeditionary Force. Slowly as autumn 1939 gave way to that freezing winter of 1940, York settled back into its old, almost peacetime-like sleep. Of course, there was some discussion of the whole issue of the war. Dr Temple, the rotund Archbishop of York, who still affected the old-fashioned clerical gaiters, felt it had been right to go to war. Still, he contended, it was *not* right to pray for victory. The new war, although a righteous one, was not a holy war.

Not far away from his beloved Minster, the Yorkshire Conservative Club, housed in neo-Gothic splendour in their Lendal Club, sat down to their 21st annual dinner that February to dine off: 'Grape fruit cocktail or *hors d'oeuvre*; a clear turtle soup or cream of chicken; fillet of sole *bonne femme*; roast saddle of Scotch mutton; baked potatoes; sprouts; orange sorbet; roast pheasant; Marasschino ice pudding; Scotch woodcock; dessert; coffee'.

Total war in York, circa February 1940! But the day would come when that same Conservative Club would count itself fortunate if it could serve its members a Woolton Pie (named after Dr Woolton, the Minister of Food) and a monstrosity of a fish, known as 'snoek'.

Propaganda. Constant appeals to save, collect, avoid waste, were showered down on a hard-pressed nation by the Ministry of Information.

The balloon, as the parlance of the time had it, went up in June 1940. Suddenly the *Wehrmacht* was surging towards the Channel ports. Belgium was knocked out of the war on the Allied side. Hastily the British Expeditionary Force retreated towards the sea. The Franco-British alliance started to fall apart.

'BLOODY MARVELLOUS!' the *Daily Mirror* headlined the great pick-up of British troops from Dunkirk. Abruptly a new man was at the helm. Winston Churchill had taken over from the discredited Neville Chamberlain.

The old man, who had come in from the cold to direct the affairs of the almost defeated nation, did not pull his punches. He told the Commons on June 6th 1940, four years to the day before British troops would return to France, that 'wars are not won by evacuation'. Dunkirk, he said, represented a 'colossal military disaster'. Still, almost single-handed, he attempted to rally the shaken nation. 'We shall fight in the fields and in the streets, we shall fight in the hills; we shall never surrender!'

His generals were not so sanguine. In a top secret conference that month held at the York Station Hotel and chaired by Anthony Eden, the Vice-Chief of the Imperial General Staff, Dill, told the politician that the Army was 'demoralised ... and may not be steady when the time comes'. The other generals agreed. The regular army would fight on if the Gerrmans invaded, even if they had to do so from far-away Canada. Not the wartime conscripts, however. They would desert to their families *en masse*.

The citizens of York knew nothing of the pessimism of the top brass, meeting in secret in their midst, of course, that summer. But they did know the pressing urgency of the new situation, with the Germans triumphant everywhere on the Continent and Britain now 'going it alone'.

Overnight the World War One tank which had been displayed since 1918 in the square facing the Theatre Royal, vanished, as did the cannon from the Boer War next to it in the King's Manor's garden. Even the vintage muzzle-loaders from the Crimean War on Blue Bridge at the Foss confluence disappeared overnight. The country was desperate for scrap to replace the weapons lost in France.

Railings disappeared from public places everywhere. Private homeowners volunteered to surrender theirs (Were they unpatriotic then, those whose railings still survive, one wonders.) Little boys roamed the streets collecting aluminium kettles and pans to 'make Spitfires for Lord Beaverbrook', the new head of the armaments industry.

London was blitzed for nearly four months, night after night, week in, week out. Harrassed officials from the 'council' toured great estates such as Kingsway trailing behind them grubby little kids from the East End, with labels around their necks. Evacuees, and all of them bed-wetters and flea-ridden, or so local opinion had it. Sandbags went up in the city centre. Most windows were adorned with strips of brown paper to reduce the effects of blast. 'Dig for Victory' gardens appeared in the most unlikely places. Even out at RAF Linton, the ground crew 'erks' started planting vegetables. Only York's treasured bowling greens remained sacrosanct.

Now at night, people living to the east of the city could see the pale flickering flames of the fires burning in Hull on the horizon, a ghastly reminder that while York had so far been spared, the port was taking 'some hammering'. When would it be the ancient city's turn, they asked themselves tensely?

A group of school kids playing on Clifton Ings among the anti-glider traps (great stakes with steel wires stretched between them) and the trenches dug by the newly formed Home Guard, saw the German plane first. 'It circled and circled against the perfect blue sky,' one of them recalled over 40 years later, 'and not a single shot was fired at it. Was it a reconnaissance plane spotting for the coming German attack, we asked ourselves? Were they on their way?'

But as that beautiful summer passed and the Battle of Britain was fought in the south, they didn't come. 1940 gave way to 1941. The face of the city was changing now. The Poles had appeared, all clicking heels and hand-kisses; very gallant men indeed, especially with the ladies. The evacuees returned to London and their

A painting of York about the time of the raid,
showing troops of all nationalities on leave in the city.
The Minster still towers triumphantly over the ancient bombed city.

former billets in Crombie Avenue, Kingsway, and the like were filled with happy-go-lucky Canadian airmen. One day there would be a whole group of them, RCAF's Sixth Group.

Betty's Café started to get a fast reputation, with the free-spending Canadian air crews, who might well die violently on the morrow, wanting to live - and live fast! Good girls didn't go to Betty's any more.

It was a terrible time. Defeat after defeat. The York men went – Africa, Asia, the Middle East – and never returned, by their scores, the hundreds, in the end by the thousand. York men were fighting – and dying – now on three continents.

There were the first scattered raids on the city. They caused little damage. Once the gas works was hit and pressure went down for a week. The housewives eking out miserable meals with a shilling's worth of meat per person, per week, perhaps and the loathed dried egg, complained. The school kids didn't mind. If the 'All clear' didn't sound by midnight, they had the following morning off school.

Russia came into the war. Churchill made his 'pact with the Devil' and Russia was now Britain's ally. She was no longer alone. Pearl Harbor and abruptly the 'Yanks' were in, 'over-paid, over-fed, over-sexed and over-here!' the locals quipped. But they were glad to have them as allies, all the same. 'Have yer got any gum, chum?' became the kids' phrase of the day. The Yanks were 'o-kay!'

A Nunthorpe schoolboy spotted the first of them just outside York station. Two of them, dressed like officers although they were enlisted men, lounging against the wall, chewing gum, while an enraged British military policeman stared at them impotently. You could almost feel him thinking: '*By God, I'd just love to run this shower inside!*' But he couldn't.

* * *

High Petergate, 1942. Note the way the policeman carries his respirator on his back.

York in 1942. With petrol rationing, traffic was no problem as can be seen from this picture of Ousebridge. Although there are plenty of people on foot in the streets, there is only one car to be seen on the bridge.

Now it seemed to the average citizen of the old city that there had never been a time without the war. It appeared to have gone on for ever.

Yet all the same the war was strangely remote from the ancient city. The war was the sole subject of headlines in the *Yorkshire Evening Press*, now reduced to four pages, the upper class Oxbridge accents of the BBC announcers reading out the news on the 'Home Service'; the Hollywood 'war pictures' at the *Grand*, the *Clifton*, the *Rialto*; the knock-about style of Mr Scott-Walker excitedly commenting in the newsreels – 'before the big picture' – on 'knocking the Hun for six' and 'whacking the Wop'.

Indeed the actual shooting war had touched York so little in three years since 1939 that the Home Office had ordered an enquiry into the costs of the city's civil defence. More, its chief Mr A. Cooke, head of the Civil Defence Organisation, the youngest in the whole of the United Kingdom, had recently been called up and was currently 'square-bashing' in the Armoured Corps training depot at Warminster. The greatest war in history seemed to have passed York by.

* * *

Jane. This was what York was reading in the Daily Mirror in 1942. Jane, the heroine of a hundred adventures, baring all once again for the cause.

*A smart flight of new entrants to the Women's Auxiliary Air Force – WAAFs,
later changed to the Women's Royal Air Force – marching in York.*

It was Tuesday, 28th April, 1942. A grey day in a grey time. York had had 790 such days already. It seemed to the average citizen of York a day like any other. A 12 hour shift at the factory (for both men and women) perhaps and then, after a quick tea (beans-on-toast, jam-on-bread and a cup of unsweetened tea – the sugar ration was two ounces per person, per week) on duty once more with the Home Guard, Fire Watching Service, Observer Corps, ARP, and half a dozen other such organisations.

For the few who had time to do so – and there were only a few, for nearly every fit male and female between the ages of 16 and 60 had been conscripted into some job or other – the *Yorkshire Evening Press* offered little that was new or encouraging. *'Fuel rationing proposed in the House . . . US Gift to York. City received from US Red Cross, huge cases of new and second-hand clothing . . .'* For those off duty and inclined to brave the strict blackout, the *Press* advertised that the Theatre Royal was showing *Bird in the Hand* described as a 'charming comedy' by John Drinkwater. At the Co-op they were offering 'strict tempo' dancing, none of this new 'jive' and 'boogie-woogie' stuff recently imported from the USA. The films at the cinemas were not very exciting either. Clifton Cinema was showing a rather sombre version of a Remarque novel – *So Ends the Night!* Indeed the only cheerful film on offer that April night was the zany, knock-about comedy *Hellsapoppin* at the Electric.

Members of the American women's services,
WACs walking equally smartly and arousing interest later in the war.

For those who were going to put their feet up this night and listen to the radio, the Home Service would feature 'The Brains' Trust' at peak listening time, while the Forces Service would counter with 30 minutes of good rousing organ music in 'Sandy's Half-Hour'. All very routine and normal.

Only one thing struck a slightly discordant note for the readers of the *Press* that night so long ago. It was the evening paper's leader. The unsigned editorial comment was entitled *'Reprisals'* and its warning was crystal clear. 'The air raids on Bath,' it read, 'followed by the raid on Norwich, remind us of the need to "keep our powder dry" on the ARP "Front", Any night any place may be expected to face a strenuous test of its preparedness and the stamina of its citizens, who, if they are wise, will not lay too much stress on their hitherto surprisingly consistent "run of luck"'.

That unknown local journalist did not know just how close he had come to the truth when he had penned his article earlier on that Tuesday. York's 'run of luck' had, after nearly three years of war, finally run out.

As the blackout descended on the city this April evening like a shroud, and the street noises died away, its citizens whether at work or at home prepared for another night of war. So far the city had had 780 alerts and nothing very much had happened. "Jerry's forgotten York', they told each other as the

GUILDHALL, YORK

In 1942 this was the oldest surviving Guildhall in England, for London's had been destroyed the previous year. Ironically, York citizens had just raised the money to put a new roof on the 500 year-old building, and in April the roof and much more were to be destroyed.

hours ticked by in leaden silence. Tomorrow would be yet another grey day, little different from this one. Little did they know that on the morrow the city would be dramatically transformed, in some parts savagely changed and barely recognisable. Soon now, *York's longest night would commence.*

THE FACE OF WAR, 1942
This was what the war meant to York's children that year. Gas mask drills, air raid drills.
Soon the drill would turn into a grim reality.

THREE: The Longest Night

'I saw across the road on the grass verge, one of her plimsolls and some of her books . . . Had she been at school . . . she would have been blown to pieces and no trace of her left.'

York woman standing outside the wreck of her daughter's school, April 29th, 1942.

MIDNIGHT!

YORK slept. The pubs and cinemas had long been closed. The BBC was silent. The soldiers from Strensall and the airmen from the airfields which surrounded the city, who had come into York to find whatever pleasures, forbidden or otherwise, were offered by the place, had long departed in their buses from Exhibition Square, hastening to their camps before 12 o'clock.

Here and there a few people were still awake. At their post in Scarcroft Road, the on-duty ARP men were strangely reluctant to sleep, although most of them had had a long day's work behind them. Finally, one of them, a part-time musician and insurance agent, put the thoughts of most of them into words, 'Lads,' he announced, 'I've a funny feeling that we're gonna cop it tonight.' The others agreed and in the end they settled down in their bunks, minus their boots, but fully dressed. It was well they did so.

* * *

ATTACKS
(Above) Bombed up and ready to go.

(Left) Oberfeldwebel Hans Fruehauf,
one of the attackers here seen in Russia.

DEFENDERS
But where were they on the night of April 28/29?
Many York citizens asked this question.

On the other side of the river at that moment, three men walked down Bootham. The street was bathed in the icy white light of a full moon and their shoes echoed hollowly on the uneven flags. In spite of the lateness of the hour and the grimness of the time, the three of them were in a happy mood. They had enjoyed a rare treat that night – a bottle of whisky – and all of them felt mellow, if sleepy.

Pausing outside the gates of St Peter's School, its headmaster, who was one of the trio, joked, 'It would be a lovely night for a reprisal raid, wouldn't it, Innes?'

The city coroner, Colonel Innes Ware, an old soldier who had fought in France in the 'other war', groaned, *'Please,'* he moaned, 'I'd like to get a good night's sleep tonight.' As Bootham's Head Air Raid Warden he had lost a lot of sleep of late.

For a minute or two more, the three of them chatted on, then they said goodnight and went their separate ways. Now Bootham was deserted, bathed in that cold light.

* * *

The price of the Raid: 300 dead and seriously injured, one-third of York's housing destroyed and damaged.

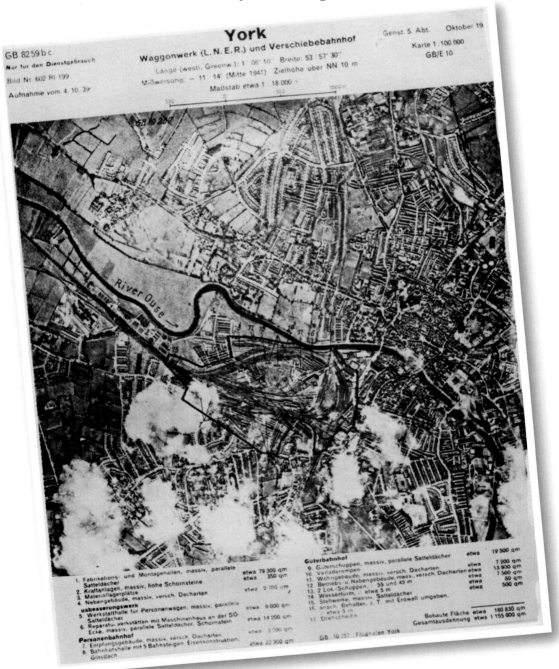

TARGET
The original German target map, taken in 1941, which was used to plan the raid.
It specifically mentions the L.N.E.R. carriage works and shunting yard. This map was
brought back to York after the war by a former employee of Rowntrees Cocoa Works.

But at Penn House, quite close to the house where Auden, the poet, had been born, Miss Grace Jenkins still could not sleep, in spite of the lateness of the hour. Recently she had undergone a serious operation and she was upset still. She stared out of the unblacked-out window at the 18th century house in the park opposite, silhouetted a stark black in the moon's light, and told herself that this was what her brother, who flew with the RAF, called a 'bomber's moon'. Abruptly she was seized by a strange sense of apprehension and foreboding. Something was going to happen . . .

* * *

They came zooming in from the east. At 200 mph. Twenty of them in two waves. The 'flying pencils' – the Junker 88s – were in the lead. Behind them came the slower Heinkel IIIs.

Flamborough Head loomed up. As one, the pilots rose to gain height. For they had flown low over the North Sea to avoid being detected by British radar. The East Riding, the broad acres of Yorkshire, flew beneath them. Down there were the Free Frenchmen, the Poles, the Canadians, the Britons, the Americans and men of another half dozen Allied nations, who would one day carry the war into Germany. But this night it was the Germans who were still attacking.

They spotted the silver snake of the Ouse on which they had been briefed hours before. It would lead them to their target. Suddenly *Oberfeldwebel* Hans Fruehauf, an observer-gunner in one of the Junkers, just back from a tour on the Russian front, saw the great silver mass of a huge church 'sticking right into the sky'. It was only later that he was informed that he had been the first to spot York Minster. 'It was beautiful, standing there above the city bathed in the cold moonlight,' he recalled many years later, 'and so close I felt I could almost lean out and touch it.'

But as below the codeword 'PURPLE' was flashed to York's Civil Defence HQ, located behind the Guildhall, Fruehauf forgot about the beauty of the scene. For already the first 'Christmas Trees', as the *Luftwaffe* crews called their massed flares, were beginning to sail down on a still sleeping York. Soon the bombs would follow. The attack had begun.

* * *

Violet Rogers, an assistant at York's celebrated Kirk Museum, was startled into wakefulness by an 'unpleasant thud' somewhere nearby in Clifton. In that same instant the sirens started to shrill their chill warning. She sprang out of bed, telling herself it had happened at last.

Hastily she dressed, grabbed her steel helmet and sought her friend Dr Alice Lewis, who also worked at the museum. They looked at the time. It was 2.30. They pelted down the stairs to find their landlord Mr Jack calmly ushering his family into the cellar.

But there was no shelter for the two young women. They had duties to perform. Outside it was as 'bright as day'. An incendiary was burning, in a brilliant white incandescent flame, in the garden and more were exploding, with a spurt of flame and a soft plop, all around. But they had no time for firebombs. They were the job of fire watchers. They had to reach their post in Alderman Morrell's house, facing Lumley Barracks, in Burton Stone Lane.

Together they ran down the road, which was 'lit up by the strange unnatural glare of magnesium from the incendiaries burning on the roofs everywhere.' They rushed into the outhouse which was their duty station to find the rest of their comrades at the First Aid Post already lying on the floor 'like sardines' and the calm Scottish voice of Dr Moss repeating over and over again, 'Lie down, lassies, while ye have a chance.'

It was a portent of what was to come.

* * *

Now the attacking Germans were scattering the Clifton-Bootham area with firebombs, lighting up the target for the high explosive to come, which would spread the flame and hopefully create one of those dreaded 'fire storms': a wall of flame heated to 1,000°C, which would sweep everything away in front of it.

Miss Jenkins, in Penn House, who had been so apprehensive, now saw that the gardens of the hospital opposite were 'ablaze with lights, just like fairy lights. It was fascinating, almost beautiful'. But it was a deadly kind of beauty. Soon men would die only yards from where she stared fascinated.

* * *

Colonel Innes Ware left his wife to the task of shepherding the children, the black Labrador Bruce, and their billetees into the cellar. Although he had received no 'purple' from the Chief Controller at the Guildhall, T. C. Benfield, to alert him, he was old soldier enough to know that this was the real thing. Now 'like soldiers going into battle for the first time', York's 1,000-odd wardens were going into action and he was needed urgently at 'Post D-One', otherwise known as Bootham Grange.

Grabbing his cycle, he set off pedalling furiously down Bootham. Opposite, his old friend's school was ablaze. Both housemasters' houses had been struck by incendiaries. Innes Ware didn't stop, he reasoned that his deputy Mr Colman would have alerted the National Fire Service.

Now he exerted all his strength, with firebombs dropping the whole length of the noble Georgian street. With nine months' of experience as a battery commander on the Menin Road in Belgium in World War One behind him, he knew that the firebombs would be followed by high explosive. He *had* to get to his post before they came whistling down.

* * *

41

YORK GUILDHALL ABLAZE
(Above) The famous building mentioned in the Baedeker tourist guidebook Hitler used to select targets for the reprisal raids in response to similar raids on Germany.

The Guildhall roof (left) was soon ablaze and burning embers quickly spread the flames to the whole of the interior. The scene from above the Guildhall next morning.

Before he could reach D-One, however, Mr. Colman had already started on his first patrol. 'He was an eager one, see,' another veteran of World War One in France, ex-warden Mr. Hatfield remembered many years later. 'We couldn't stop him, whatever we said. He wanted to see what was going on'.

Unfortunately Mr. Colman didn't get far. There was the shriek of the first high explosive bomb. Ware flung himself to the ground 100 yards away. The stick of bombs dropped with a frightening series of crashes. Under him the ground swayed and trembled. They straddled the little railway bridge linking Grosvenor Terrace and Bootham Terrace. Mr. Colman fell, killed instantly by a piece of shrapnel.

* * *

Not far away, in that instant, a lone fire team was trying to set up its pump to put out the flames in a burning Bootham. Driver E. Fox volunteered to man the pump while his mate Arthur Broadhead ran to check if the hose was correctly attached to the hydrant. Later Mr. Fox, the lucky one, recalled: 'I was watching the pipe filling with water when there was an almighty bang and I was flung to the ground. A bomb had fallen between the pump and me. A small piece of shrapnel had caused a very superficial wound to my leg. Arthur Broadhead was blown to pieces.'

Later he was identified by a signet ring attached to a little finger, all that was ever found of him. The raid had claimed its first two victims. They were not going to be the last.

* * *

Oberfeldwebel Fruehauf recognised the railway station as his pilot turned for his second run. They had been well briefed on the elegant Victorian station. They had been told if they could knock it out, they would paralyse the London-and-North-Eastern's traffic throughout the north-east, in particular, on the coast. 'Rub out the signalling system,' the briefing officer had informed them, 'and there won't be much leaving Hull for Murmansk to help the Russians for the next weeks!' Fruehauf, who had just returned from the *Ostfront* knew just how much help his comrades there needed to stop the 'Ivans'. He concentrated on the curved glass roofs of the enemy station, bathed in the glare of flares and fires, as they loomed ever larger. *This was it.*

* * *

The crowded 10.15 pm express had just steamed into the station from London as the sirens started to shrill their warning. Immediately the loudspeakers located next to the big clock sprang into action. That 'cut-glass voice', as the locals had always called it, now hurried and excited, warned all passengers to vacate the train and take cover. Assistant Station Master Mr. Lyon and Inspector Skelton of the Railway Police ran along the blackout packed express repeating the warning.

But the weary servicemen who had fought for places in King's Cross station over five hours before, many of them laden down with rifle, steel helmet, and full Field Service Marching Order, complete with kitbag, were not going to relinquish their places. After all, this was York, not much blitzed London, and most of them had another 200 miles to Edinburgh still in front of them. They stayed put.

The first 250 pound bomb crashed down and, exploding at the far end of the station, sending the station's glass roof raining down, changed all that. Madly the servicemen and the few civilians on the train scrambled for cover just as the next stick hit the station. One bomb exploded near the parcels office, followed an instant later by a shower of spluttering incendiary bombs. In a flash, everything was ablaze, including the wooden roof joists, the main track – and the 10.15 express from London.

Why York Station?
York Station in wartime was part of an important junction through which armaments and essential war material passed on its way to Hull. From there the vitally needed supplies went to the Russian port of Murmansk. The bombing of the station certainly put a stop to that traffic for a short time. Next morning the chaos looked formidable; but in fact traffic was very quickly restored to almost normal.

THE END OF THE LINE
(below) for the famous A4 Pacific locomotive 'Sir Ralph Wedgwood', lying in the
devastated York running sheds on the morning after the raid.
Damage to Platforms 1, 2 and 3 was extensive (above),

Mr. Lyon, two shunters, and an unknown soldier sprang into action. While the station staff ran to tackle the blaze with primitive stirrup pumps, Lyon doubled down the littered platform, its length showered with blazing debris from the roof. Somehow, working feverishly, he managed to divide the train. Hastily, two shunter drivers backed out of the burning station with 14 coaches, leaving the remaining six burning fiercely on the track.

*Five nuns were killed when a high explosive bomb landed directly on
the corner of the Bar Convent School building in Nunnery Lane.*

Now while the women porters in their baggy blue overalls kicked burning firebombs from the platform onto the rails, Signalman Simpson, whose signal box had been damaged by the bomb blast, swung himself into the cab of a shunter

The remains (above) of Nos. 19 & 21 Nunthorpe Grove after the raid, in contrast with the happy scene (right) at No. 19 a short time before it.

and with it clattered into action. He linked up the burning parcel van on Number 15 platform and steamed out of the station towing 20 coaches and vans behind him.

Meanwhile the platform staff had not been idle. Booking office staff and volunteers set about, dragging blazing office furniture across the debris-littered road into the safety of the moat opposite. Two fire-watchers scooped up all the money in the booking office tills and wondered for a moment, as firebombs fell all around, how to transport it to safety. Then one of them had a bright idea. He picked up the Wellington boots of passenger agent William Green. Hastily he poured the money into the left one. With the precious boot clutched to his chest, he fled to the safety of the Station Hotel. The L.N.E.R. would not make a loss on this raid!

* * *

Now the German attackers concentrated their full fury on the main line that ran in and out of York Station. Inevitably, non-military targets to left and right of the line suffered. Bar Convent School, a hundred yards from the Station, was hit, the bomb slicing through the tall austere building immediately behind the Georgian façade. All the boarders had long taken to the cellars. One old nun had been unable do so. Now Mother Gerard, the Mother superior, and Sister Patricia went to the old nun's aid. They were killed immediately and a further three nuns trapped in the smoking debris.

Bar Convent was not the only school hit. Manor High Grade School was totally destroyed. Poppleton Road received a direct hit. Shipton Street, Queen Anne's,

Nunthorpe, Bootham, St. Peter's (where ironically the greatest fire-raiser of all, Guy Fawkes, had been educated), were all damaged or burning.

The bomb which had damaged Nunthorpe School had landed only yards away at No 19 Nunthorpe Grove. The home of Mr and Mrs Blakeborough had been demolished and the survivors, who were ATS girls stationed at Fulford Barracks, were reported trapped beneath the wreckage. Immediately the Scarcroft Road team went into action. That same insurance agent, who had voiced the fears of all his comrades, now found himself tunnelling deep into the wreckage, wondering 'if the ruddy lot might fall on me at any moment!' He spotted a hand, 'a little white girl's hand'. He stretched out and started to tug while his mates held on to his feet. The girl emerged, dead, or so he thought.

Later her mother, Mrs. Blakeborough was dragged out, a great gaping wound in her head which would keep her in hospital for six months. As for the missing ATS girl, she was found nine days later *drowned* in the water of the fire pumps which had collected in the hollow in that section of Nunthorpe Grove.

It was only 42 years later that the

Five York people owed their lives to this Morrison shelter (top) still standing in the ruins after the raid. In 1941 such shelters became part of the furniture (above) for people in vulnerable areas.

rescuer, now 81 years of age, learned that the little girl *hadn't* died that terrible night, after all. She had survived to go to America and marry an American surgeon. But her mother still bore the scar of that night on her forehead, carefully hidden beneath her curls; she bore it to the grave: a tangible memento to her bravery and fortitude during York's longest night.

* * *

But in the midst of all the horror and tragedy, there were moments of humour. The Rev. Harry Radcliffe, curate of St. Olave's, was wandering around the wreckage in Bootham in his capacity as air raid warden, when an irate voice snapped, 'Get off me bloody legs!' Flashing his torch down, the reverend gentleman could just make out a figure under the rubble. 'Bloody well hurry up and get me out!' the trapped man demanded. Rev. Radcliffe did his best, frantically digging at the bricks and masonry with his hands to 'free the old codger who didn't have a word of thanks to say to me for my efforts.' Later when the parson went to pay for a well-deserved cup of tea at the mobile canteen, he discovered that 'the old codger, while I'd been pulling him out with all my might – had nicked my wallet!'

* * *

Not far away from where the Reverend Radcliffe was making that discovery, Colonel Ware was busy trying to organise a fire-fighting party to fight a blaze in The Avenue. The women of the ATS who had been billeted in the burning house started to drag out a hose, but Colonel Ware, a gentleman of the old school, thought the job much too dangerous for the girl-soldiers. Instead he climbed onto the roof of the house himself, dragging the hose behind. Finally he managed to get into position and cried to the girls below, '*Water on!*' He tensed to take the pressure. All he got for his efforts was a rude belch of hot air. In their haste the ATS had attached the hose incorrectly. The house continued to burn.

* * *

But it was not only Innes Ware who was having trouble with the Army. His wife, a resolute lady, emerged from her cellar nearby, her face blackened with soot, Bruce the dog, his coat turned white in a matter of an hour, with her canary singing crazily in the chaos of her living room, to find a Signals Corps captain billeted on her, fumbling wildly with his service revolver. 'What on earth are you doing?' she demanded.

'They say Jerry drops parachutists during the cover of a raid,' the captain explained excitedly. 'I'm going out to shoot them.' 'Put that gun away,' Mrs Ware commanded firmly. She looked around grimly at her shattered room and snapped, 'The way I feel at this moment – if any German parachutist lands here, I'll strangle him personally – *with my own bare hands!*'

* * *

But Ware's wardens were suffering now. Since Mr. Colman's death in Bootham, a further two wardens Mr. A. Emmerson and Mr. H. Fowler had been killed outright by the same bomb. But not only the wardens. 'Incidents', as they were called in the officialese of the time, were flooding in from all sides. *'Four trapped Queen Anne's Road'* . . . *'Mother killed baby in arms Water Lane'* . . . *'Bomb dropped St Olave's Road . . . severe damage'* . . . . *'Clifton Aerodrome severely damaged . . . Night guard wiped out . . .'* Nearly every street, from Kingsway through Crombie Avenue, round via Rowntrees Bridge, through the maze of terraced streets along the railway line, right up Grosvenor Terrace, and back into Bootham once more, all were now reporting death and destruction as the Germans pressed home their attack relentlessly and without any opposition.

The pupils of the Blind School, situated in the King's Manor, had filed out in pathetic obedience to the first sirens, a line of sightless boys and girls. Now deep in the bowels of the ancient medieval building, they could smell burning. They knew that something was seriously wrong, but they could do nothing about it. So they waited stoically, not knowing that both their own school and the Art Gallery next door were on fire. The six fire-watchers of the Army Pay Corps who occupied the building had been unable to deal with the blaze. Now the city's cultural pride, the Art Gallery, was burning merrily.

Across the road, two firemen, ignoring the bombs falling close by, had linked their hose through the stage door of the Theatre Royal and were spraying the roofs of the Education Department (in St Leonard's) and the other local government offices across the way in Duncombe Place with water, trying desperately to put out the fires caused by the incendiaries.

* * *

Another loss for Rowntrees. A riverside warehouse which was wrecked in the raid, being cleared up two weeks later.

(Above) The entrance to the Guildhall on the morning after the raid.

Now all was controlled chaos in the city centres. Firebells jingled, dispatch riders careered around corners, desperate ARP men and soldiers crunched through broken glass and debris, hands held across their faces against the flames. Fires flickered everywhere; and all the while the German planes dived and bombed the defenceless city.

Out of the back door of the Mary Wandesford's Home in Bootham, a determined 91-year-old Mrs. Martin led the other inhabitants in a slow, frightened crocodile, past what is now BBC York, to the relative safety of Gillygate. All the old ladies remembered the Zeppelins which had flown over York in 1916, but they had seemed relatively harmless. Now in the last years of their lives, they were experiencing the full, terrifying force of modern war. But Mrs. Martin, at least, remained unafraid. Ignoring the fires all about and the shrapnel hissing lethally through the air, she set about comforting her friends, marooned in this little island of comparative safety, while the killing went on.

And above this scene of death and destruction towered the Minster, its wall coloured a blood red hue by the fires all around, looking to some that terrible morning like a symbol of the ancient city's ability to survive.

* * *

A YMCA tea car served the firemen at work in Coney Street.

In 1940, London's celebrated Guildhall had been gutted and destroyed. Thereafter, York's own 500-year old Guildhall had become the oldest in the country. Now it – and the whole of Coney Street – came under attack. Firebombs showered down. Almost at once, its splendid roof (which had replaced the old one, ravaged by time and the deathwatch beetle, by public subscription in 1939) was set on fire. The church of St. Martin-le-Grand and the nearby Press offices were also soon ablaze. Across the river opposite, a Rowntrees warehouse, said to be filled with sugar, was hit and began to blaze fiercely.

Desperately the firemen from Malton tried to fight the fires which had broken out not only in Coney Street, but in New Street, Davygate, in the Leopard Arcade, while stretcher-bearer parties from Rowntrees doubled back and forth, carrying away the casualties. But the firemen were fighting a losing battle. The roof on the Guildhall came crashing down bringing with it more danger, as it disintegrated on the marble floor below, scattering burning debris everywhere. The nearby church of St. Martin's was in equally bad shape. The west window shattered. Pieces of glass illustrating the life of the saint after whom the medieval church had been named showered the hard-pressed firemen who were now attempting to tackle a new blaze at the city's Central Post Office, only feet away from the key

York Station. Another view of the aftermath.

ARP control unit. If the harassed Controller T. C. Benfield lost touch with his 1,000 man strong organisation, chaos would follow.

* * *

Now the Germans made their last determined attack to knock out the station and the surrounding yards, knowing just how important it was to their comrades – 'the stubble-hoppers', as the weary German infantrymen called themselves – on the Russian front.

This time they used high explosive, showering the area of the Carriage Works with bombs. One struck the 'roundhouse' where 20 locomotives were parked around the central turntable. In an instant the place was a shambles. Every locomotive was scarred or ripped by shrapnel, with three of them seriously damaged. They included the L.N.E.R.'s pride, an A-4 streamlined Pacific locomotive, ironically enough named after an ex-Chairman of the Railway Executive Committee *Sir Ralph Wedgwood*. Now the wrecked *Sir Ralph* was tossed on its side like a thrown away child's toy.

But not only the railway's 'iron horses' suffered. Racing across the site of the present day National Railway Museum, the German bombers dropped a stick near the Leeman Road stables which housed the L.N.E.R.'s drayhorses. One of the bombs hit the stables. They started to burn fiercely.

Immediately Stableman Alfred Martin, accompanied by Van-Setter H. Crave and Police Constable A. Asquith, rushed in to free the terrified horses. Ignoring the Shires' and Clyedesdales' flailing hooves, as the animals lashed out in their

The road to school. Rubble and rescue trucks block the entrance to Queen Anne Road on the following morning. Fires lower down the street are still burning, and firemen play their hoses over the smoking shells of the buildings.

terror at the mounting flames, Martin loosened their halters, urging them out of the burning stables with a hearty slap on their massive rumps. One by one they were led to safety, until the sweating threesome, their faces blackened with smoke, had freed 19 of them. But the rescue operation had had a price. Mr. Martin's prized 'dig for victory' garden had been ruined. The panic-stricken horses had churned it up with their hooves. At that moment Mr. Martin, a passionate gardener, was saddened more by the loss of his ruined garden than by that of his burning house.

* * *

Over at the station, they were fighting frantically to keep the system working. Now the casualties were mounting, two dead and many more wounded or injured. Blacksmith V. J. Hudson carried on fighting the flames, although he had suffered a fractured leg, until he collapsed. Foreman A. Cade was only snatched from certain death at the last moment by Porter A. Hunter. The situation was growing desperate. While the fire-fighters continued their struggle, Works Superintendent Mr. Love tried to get the lines cleared for the morrow's vital war

As dawn broke, the city was covered in smoke and the streets were strewn with rubble.

traffic. The army was contacted. They reported that Engineers were already on their way to help out at the station. From Fulford, itself under attack, Divisional Manager Mr. Charles Jones was speeding though the burning streets to take charge. But even as he fought his way to the crippled centre, he realised that not only was the North-Eastern railway system in serious trouble, but that the main access roads would soon be blocked. That dawn a group of bombed-out children and women from Hull on their way to York were stopped by the police at Beverley and were told it was no use proceeding any further in search of new accommodation in the ancient city, for *'York has been wiped off the map!'*

* * *

Of course, it wasn't true. All the same, from Clifton Airfield in the north-west of the city to Fulford Barracks in the south-east, the city was under attack, with hardly a street escaping damage, even if it was only a few roof tiles ripped off by the blast of the exploding bombs.

And casualties were mounting too. With the emergency services fully occupied now with 58 fires still raging and 67 serious 'incidents', which included at least 37 men, women and children still trapped under the wreckage, the 'walking wounded' had to look after themselves. Mrs Ezard had been on night shift when her place of work had been struck. Now she and two friends who had suffered facial burns took advantage of a sudden lull in the bombing to crunch their way over broken glass to the County Hospital for treatment. But the halls and wards were packed with seriously wounded people, lying moaning on stretchers, waiting for treatment. They decided their injuries weren't *that* serious. They left untreated.

At the Morrell House's First Aid Post, its windows now shattered, some of the roof gone, a steaming brown bomb crater in the garden like the work of some gigantic mole, Violet Rodgers and her friend Dr. Alice Lewis from the Kirk Museum worked steadily trying to cope with the casualties, most of them from Burton Stone Lane and Bootham Crescent. Most of the injuries were minor, but there were stretcher cases too. Dr. Moss went from patient to patient, hastily stitching them up, bandaging the white-faced shocked elderly ladies, with a quick word and an encouraging pat for each.

Some needed no encouragement in spite of the ordeal they had just been through. Mrs. Sachs emerged from the wreck of her own house, with a blanket thrown over her dust-covered clothes. This dawn it was the only thing she now possessed. But she did not let that daunt her. She knew that now the city would be filled with hungry, homeless people just like her. So she hurried to the 'British Restaurant' in Aldwark, which had been set up by the Ministry of Food to ensure that working people had one good, cheap, hot meal a day. Here she was catering manageress and now she got the place going immediately to provide food for the homeless and the men of the ARP.

By the end of the week, directing 24-hour shifts, she would serve a colossal 14,000 lunches, 2,800 breakfasts and 2,800 teas! In the next seven days, 1,640lbs of bread alone would have been consumed. Later Mrs. Sachs would tell the *Press* that the chef, Mr. Martin, who was on the verge of collapse from overwork, 'deserved a medal'. Many thought that week that she deserved one herself.

* * *

Trooper Cooke, on his first leave since he had been called up, rushed to the hard-pressed Control Centre next to the burning Guildhall. He asked T. C. Benfield, the harassed Controller, if he could do anything to help.

'Everything's under control,' T. C. answered. 'But you could go and see if everything's working well at the Butter Market.' He looked significantly at the much younger Cooke. 'It's a very sensitive area, you know what I mean?'

Cooke did. The Butter Market in Kent Street, near the old Cattle Market, was the city's emergency mortuary, only to be used in situations like this. It meant that the civilian populations were taking serious casualties. Thus he set off across the blazing city on his mission to arrive at the mortuary, packed with civil defence workers, funeral directors – and the dead.

Cooke had been instrumental in setting up the place. In 1939 the Government had urged councils to have supplied cheap papier-mâché coffins for emergencies such as this. But York City councillors would have nothing of it. No citizen of

SECRET AND CONFIDENTIAL.

City of York

INVASION COMMITTEE

**COMBINED
CIVIL AND MILITARY
DEFENCE SCHEME**

Guildhall
YORK
August, 1943   Y.P.W.—110—(587)—10/43.

Unless specific instructions to the contrary have been given from Control Headquarters, casualties should be disposed of as follows:-

Those requiring hospital treatment to

County Hospital, Monkgate

or

City Infirmary, Huntington Road.

(Note:- Contaminated casualties requiring hospital treatment should be sent to the City Infirmary).

Those requiring first aid post treatment (i.e. Lightly wounded and/or contaminated) :-

City Infirmary first aid post,
St. George's Baths,
The Horse Repository, Lendal Bridge.
Beckfield Lane, Acomb, first aid post.

(Note:- The Horse Repository is not yet ready for action and instructions will be issued when it is ready).

The leader of the party will decide priority of removal and give instructions for the ambulance to return for further loads if necessary. He should see that casualties are sheltered pending the return of the ambulance vehicles, and should notify Control Headquarters if he considers that further assistance is necessary.

Marking of casualties

First aid parties are not expected to label all casualties or take names and addresses.

It is essential, however, that labels be used and the casualty marked in the following circumstances:-

If a tourniquet has been applied	"T" on the forehead and on the label.
If morphia has been given (e.g. when a doctor has been present)	"M" on the forehead and on the label, and if possible a fraction indicating the dose. Thus "M½" would indicate ½ grain.
If haemorrhage is present	"H" on the forehead and on the label.
Wounds of the chest and/or abdomen	"X" on the forehead and on the label.
If gas contaminated	"C" on the forehead and on the label.

GRIMLY PRACTICAL
Instructions issued to those who had the task of coping with the effects of attack from the air, recognizing the stark realities of what they were likely to face.

DEAD

During air raids many people are killed outright, and it is the duty of rescue and first aid parties to dispose suitably of bodies before finally leaving the spot. Bodies should be taken to the nearest available building or other shelter and if possible covered over. Personal belongings should, whenever possible, be kept with the body. The numbers and exact disposition of bodies should be reported to the leader of the party to the Officer in Charge of the depot immediately on return. It is, of course, essential that all members of the parties are satisfied that a person is dead and if the slightest doubt exists appropriate treatment should be given until a doctor has stated that death is present.

Equipment

Each member of the party is responsible for seeing that his pouch has a full complement of equipment, and that his water bottle is full of fresh drinking water. Expended materials should be reported to the leader of the party. The leader of the party is responsible for seeing that the haversack has a full complement of equipment.

The instructions given above should be read carefully by all members of first aid parties, and all are asked to bear in mind that by individual courtesy, tact and initiative an efficient service will be built up.

You are playing a vital part in your City's Civil Defence Scheme - your fellow citizens are relying on you to play that part efficiently and intelligently.

the ancient city was going to be buried in 'a bit o' cheap paper'. So Cooke had devised a scheme whereby every undertaker in the city would keep two coffins in reserve for air raid victims.

Now as Cooke entered he saw that there would be need of them. The emergency mortuary had been divided into three departments, a waiting room, a little makeshift chapel, and the 'bodies' room. Now this last lived up to its grim name. Under the leadership of a well-known York undertaker Mr. Sykes, the others of his calling were trying to sort out the mangled bloody bodies which filled the place. Even at a distance of 40-odd years, Mr. Cooke, an unemotional man, recalled they were 'pretty ghastly. One mother, dead, with her child locked in her arms, also dead, the two of them, mixed up with brick rubble lying on a metal stretcher . . . In a couple of cases, all that was needed was a bucket to put the remains in.'

Trooper Cooke, who would one day fight in Normandy and carry the war to Germany, went to work, helping with the identification of the bodies, telling himself as he did so, how typically English everything was. 'Quiet, subdued, unemotional.'

* * *

Oberfeldwebel Fruehauf's Junkers was going in for the last time. Following the line of the railway from the north, it swept in low towards the glare of the city centre. He saw a tall brick building, with a chimney stack poorly camouflaged to his left. He recognised it from the briefing photos. It was a chocolate factory – Rowntrees – and not important. The bomb aimer must have thought the same. For he dropped the first of his stick on the bridge crossing the railway line just opposite from the squat red brick factory.

Fortunately so for that part of York, for unknown to German Intelligence and most of York's citizens for that matter, the traditional anti-war Quaker family of Rowntrees (who had not liked the idea of one of their members, Captain Philip Rowntree, joining the Company's Home Guard company) had formed a new company in 1940 under the innocuous name of County Industries Ltd. Now in the one time 'gum-room', shifts of local girls no longer made fillings for chocolates. Instead they filled shell casings with high explosive. If Rowntrees had been hit at that moment, instead of the railway bridge, an unprecedented disaster might have taken place in York that night.

Suddenly Fruehauf up above the factory pressed his throat mike, '*Herr Oberleutnant*,' he rasped urgently. '*Hurricane!*'

Coming in from the port side, machine guns already chattering, white tracer zipping through the darkness, the dark shape of a night fighter was hurtling towards the much slower Junkers 88. The Tommy fighters had arrived on the scene at last!

* * *

At the age of 23 Free French Pilot Officer Yves Mahé, the pilot of one of the first Hurricanes to arrive at the scene, already had an adventurous life behind him. After the French surrender back in 1940, he had stolen a plane, just before the advancing *Boche* had taken over his base. Unknown to Yves, his flyer brother was doing the same thing, disguised as a Polish officer because his commanding officer had refused to allow him to leave France. By a roundabout route in their stolen planes, both officers had reached England in order to join de Gaulle and continue the fight. Amazingly enough on his first day in London sight-seeing, Yves had bumped into none other than his brother! Now the dark-haired

A squadron of Hurricane fighters on the lookout for German planes.

Frenchman with his trim moustache, flashed by Fruehauf's Junker and headed straight for an unsuspecting Heinkel III machine-gunning the streets below.

His first burst missed. The stream of tracer zipped by the Heinkel's tail like a myriad angry hornets. But it alerted the German pilot. He broke to the right. Grimly Mahé followed. He pinned himself to the Heinkel's tail, riddling the fuselage with tracer. The Heinkel's rear gunner attempted to fight back. To no avail. Thick black smoke was already pouring from the right engine.

'I gave the Hun a good taste of his own medicine and his fire ceased,' Mahé was quoted as saying the next day in the unfeeling prose of the time. 'I fired again and followed the Heinkel as it spiralled down, but near the ground I lost sight of it in the smoke and haze of dust that hung over the city.'

Yves Mahé had his first 'kill'. In due course General de Gaulle would kiss him on both cheeks and award him the *Croix de Guerre*. He would be given a civic welcome too at the Mansion House, complete with cucumber sandwiches.

* * *

At 1,000 feet the crew began to bail out of the crippled Heinkel. One by one their chutes opened and one by one each crew member was unlucky enough to be struck by the tail as the doomed bomber spiralled downwards. For a moment the five members blacked out. When they came to they saw to their horror they were heading straight for the Ouse where they could well drown, laden as they were with their heavy flying gear.

Desperately they fought their shroud lines and somehow managed to escape that fate. The turret gunner hit the ground first to find himself alone in enemy territory, the only sound the wind in the trees. For a while the 22-year-old German stood bewildered on the bank of the Ouse wondering what he should do next. In the end he stumped to the little collection of houses in the distance where he gave himself up.

When they questioned him, he was found to have come from Rostock, the attack on which had triggered the 'Baedeker Raids'. But he had heard nothing of the bombing from his mother who still lived there. Asked what 'do you think of Rudolf Hess?' 'Ach, dead and buried,' he snorted . . . 'dead and buried.' In fact, Rudolf Hess who had flown to Britain in 1941 was still alive decades after that unknown German had pronounced him 'dead and buried.'

* * *

That narrow escape from Mahé had been enough for Fruehauf's pilot. He jettisoned the last of his bombs 'uselessly' on both sides of the railway line leading from York to Huntington. Then he fled for the coast. He made it safely though later it was claimed that five of the 20 attackers had been knocked down. And that was the last *Oberfeldwebel* Hans Fruehauf of Wittlich on the Moselle ever saw of York. Like so many survivors of the raids on England that spring and summer, he finally ended up on the Russian front fighting on foot – *as an infantryman.*

* * *

Now it was almost over. Mr. Myers who owned a house at the corner of Seagrove Walk and Grantham Drive staggered out in a daze to find a 1,000lb bomb embedded in his garden. White-faced and shaken, he shouted at a group of wardens, 'I've got summat in my garden!'

But the wardens had more pressing problems on their hands than the thing in Mr. Myers' garden. Everywhere they were still tunnelling into the wreckage to free trapped people. In the Clifton and Burton Stone Lane area, there were nearly 20 of them. A soldier and a woman were pinned down by smoking debris next to a bomb crater. In spite of the sinister hiss of escaping gas, which might ignite at any moment, the rescue workers toiled for two hours to free the two of them. At the back of Clifton Cinema, now a bingo hall, civilian defence workers from the Foss Island Post dug frantically into a mountain of wreckage. Below somewhere there were trapped civilians. Seven hours later a weary but triumphant woman, bearing a filthy screaming baby in her arms, would be saved.

Finally, as the sky started to flush the dirty white of the false dawn, the 'all clear' sirens began to sound. From Rowntrees and Terry's, from the Waterworks, the Hull Road Printing Works, Electricity Department, Acomb Infant School and

Business as usual. The Jersey Dairy carries on in new premises, notified on the ruins of its old shop next to St. Martin-le-Grand in Coney Street.

half a dozen other places, their calm level tone indicated that the worst was over.

In the former sorting shed of the Central Post Office, Lendal, the men of the Royal Observer Corps took off their earphones and wiped sweat-lathered faces. The men, two solicitors, a plumber, a salesman and a depot manager under the supervision of Mr. T. Wilton had been hunched over a huge plotting map of the York area, taking reports from outside posts trying to assess the enemy intentions.

They had had a rough night. They had picked up the 'bandits' as soon as they had crossed Flamborough Head. An abrupt change in their direction and they had guessed immediately that York was 'for it'. They had been right.

Situated in the heart of the city at a location which was kept secret right till the end of the war, they had experienced the full impact of the bombing of Coney Street, as well as the searing heat coming from Rowntrees North Street Depot on the other side of the river, where the precious sugar stored there was still burning furiously.

Once an observer standing next to the dias near the weather board was blown six feet to land on his feet once more as a bomb exploded close by. An incendiary had crashed through the roof too. A table supervisor rushed out, extinguished it, and returned to his place without saying a word. Fighter Command, with whom they were in constant touch in that tight rickety wooden room, had reported a 'bandit' shot down and they had removed their pipes and cigarettes (they had chain-smoked throughout the raid) and cheered.

Now at 45 minutes past four they received the magic words 'observer release'. They and their isolated, freezing posts all over the Yorkshire countryside could stand down. From the 'Purple', the codeword which had alerted them, at 2.36 am, to 'White' at 4.46, they had spent exactly 120 minutes at their tense, nerve racking job.

It would be two more years before they would ever again experience anything like this. Then the whole character of the air war would have changed and on that Christmas Eve, 1944, they would no longer be plotting enemy aircraft but enemy missiles: the progress of the forerunners of our present-day cruise missiles. The 30 odd V-1s launched off the Humber by the *Kampfgruppe 53*, were aimed as a lethal Christmas present at Manchester.

But that would be in the future. Now their longest night was over and gratefully they slumped in their seats and drank the tea brought in to them in great metal pails.

* * *

Working in the dark and then among the smouldering buildings, firemen had a gruelling task. (Left) Moving into the Leopard Arcade to find the injured.

Now, slowly, the citizens of York began to emerge from their cellars and shelters to discover that the face of the ancient city had been transformed. Virtually every street in the city centre had suffered some damage. Windows were out everywhere. Many roofs were off, yards from the great gaping holes caused by the direct hits. Even today a casual observer can walk around the centre of York and spot the lighter grey tiles which were used patch up roofs 60-odd years ago; or note the opaque glass used then to repair windows (one process in the making of wartime glass was left out to speed up production). The scars are to be seen everywhere still.

Thirty years later, in an account given to the *Yorkshire Evening Press*, Violet Rogers (now Mrs. Wloch), remembered that morning of April 1942 with the freshness of almost total recall. 'Bootham was a sight to make the historical weep. Glass, glass everywhere, crunching under our feet. Every house had staring empty windows, tiles off the roof, and the walls all pitted with machine-gun bullets . . .'

But as the young museum assistant reached the end of a shattered Bootham, hosepipes with fire engines blocking its whole length, while steel-helmeted wardens attempted to restore some sort of order to the chaos she caught sight of the 'medieval pile of Bootham Bar gleaming white and undamaged in the sunlight.' For her, 'it was a symbol of endurance, the continuity between the ancient city's long past and the certainty of the future.'

The city's longest night was over, and very definitely – *Yorkshire would endure.*

(Right) Firemen at work on the ruins of St. Martin-le-Grand, Coney Street.

SURVIVORS: *Mr. and Mrs. Blakeborough still lived at No. 19, Nunthorpe Grove half a century later. 'I was away working at the carriage-works that night of the raid,' said Mr. Blakeborough, 'and when I came home I just stood and stared in disbelief at the hole that used to be my home. (See p.47). They told me that my wife and daughter were at the hospital and I rushed over there right away.' All those year later Mrs Blakeborough still carries the jagged scar on her forehead, and marvels that she is still alive. 'For a long time we did not tell her what had happened next door. It would have been too much of a shock.' Next door, at No. 21, six people had been in the house. One, a pretty ATS girl, had been up late polishing her boots ready for a parade at Fulford Barracks in the morning. When the bomb landed, all six were blown right out of the house, and by some fluke five survived. The sixth was nowhere to be seen. That was Anne, the ATS girl. Nine days later when the water-filled bomb crater was drained, her body was found.*

'That night is over, but it has left us with a proud standard for the days which lie ahead, to which we rededicate ourselves.'

The Dean of York, the Very
Rev. Milner White, D.S.O.,
May 1942

Demolished houses in the Clifton district of York.

'THE spirit of Blitz York stands very high ... Nazi fury launched at York... Nazi reprisal raid on York ... Widows gunned in hostel garden ...' Such were headlines in the local and national press the following morning as they reported the ancient city's longest night. The emphasis was on German terror and the British ability to 'carry on' and 'business as usual'.

The London *Daily Mail* featured, on its page five, a rather shaky jingle under the title *Baedeker Bombers* which proclaimed: 'We keep our history. Though buildings fall – Mansion or Minster, Monument or hall'. Not exactly great poetry by any means. But it was the kind of stuff the people at the top thought would rally people at the bottom.

The staff reporter of the *Yorkshire Observer,* one of the first on the scene the following morning, noted: 'The beautiful spires of the undamaged Minster against a blue sky ... a tired looking girl serving buns and bread over a confectionery counter – bombed out of her home six hours before – tradespeople sweeping away glass splinters into neat piles outside their shops ... the cheerful faces and the bustle of the streets'.

He continued his long article on the sights and sounds of York that next morning in the same tenor. He came across 'one woman who was bombed out and refused to leave her home until she found a duster to clean up with. Another woman who left her damaged home, noticed the statue of Napoleon had been blown against the window of a tobacconist shop it adorned so that the Little Corporal appeared to be looking down the street. "Anyway that old blighter's all right!" she called as she walked away.'

Walking through the streets of the city centre, the reporter found 'people laughing and talking about their experiences. They might have been a holiday crowd walking out in the sunshine. I have seen people looking much less happy at Blackpool'. It was all good, uplifting stuff, showing that life in York went on and its citizens were plucky and full of true Yorkshire grit.

* * *

The reality was a little different. At the Public Library, the centre of the emergency services, the WVS were beginning to post the grim lists of the dead. Within the city boundaries, there were 72; 19 men, 39 women and – sadly – 14 children, who had been killed in the bombing. Ninety-two persons had been seriously injured and 113 slightly wounded. Together with the four Civil Defence personnel killed and five soldiers aiding them (plus an unknown number of wounded), it meant that some 300 men, women, and children had paid the butcher's bill inside the city limits. To that figure has to be added 14 killed, six seriously injured and one slightly injured in Flaxton district. The RAF figures for those killed in the officers' mess and guardroom which had received direct hits at Clifton airfield were never published. Nor were the soldier casualty figures released. In addition, 9,500 houses had been damaged or destroyed in the city: roughly one third of the total of 28,000 at that time. In short, it had been the greatest blood-letting and destruction in York's recent history.

At 11 o'clock that same morning, the Regional Commision under the chairmanship of Ormsby-Gore (later Lord Harlech) met to hold the official inquest on the raid. T. C. Benfield convinced the assembled brasshats and local bigwigs that – with two exceptions (it was never revealed what they were) – York's defences had stood up well to the attack. Later in the Committee's confidential report, it was stated: "It is thought that the foregoing summary enables it to be said without hesitation that, on the whole, the services and the citizens acquitted themselves well'.

* * *

Undoubtedly the local ARP services and the citizens had. But the Armed Services patently had not. After the other Baedeker raids, it was pretty clear that it would be York's turn sooner or later. Yet when, as Mr Cooke put it, 'we found that more than 40 hostile planes, 30 miles out to sea, going north, had suddenly turned due west and were coming in over Flamborough Head, we had no doubt that York was in for it, why weren't RAF fighters waiting for them?'

Why did it take Lt. Mahé's lone night-fighter of the Free French Air Force so long to appear on the scene, so the Germans could bomb with impunity for over 90 minutes? Where were Commander of Britain's Anti-Aircraft Defences, General Pile's ack-ack guns and barrage balloons? (Ironically enough they made their appearance later when York was never again seriously threatened by conventional aircraft.)

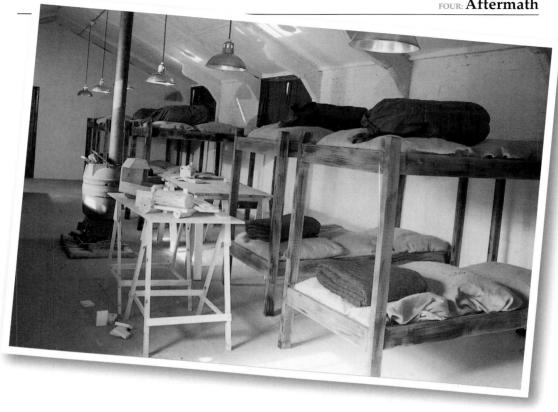

Prisoner-of-War Hut, Eden Camp, Malton, North Yorkshire

The problem of the lack of defences around York is complicated by a factor that could not be assessed until the mid-70s, 30 years later, when Group Captain Fred Winterbotham revealed the secret of Ultra: that British Intelligence was able to read orders given to German commanders by means of the Enigma coding machine almost as quickly as the German recipients themselves.

At Bletchley in the Home Counties, the first computer, known to the boffins who worked there as the 'Green Goddess', had been breaking the secrets of the Enigma since May 1940. The battle of El Alamein had been fought on the basis of these intercepts, as was the sinking of the *Bismarck* one year earlier in 1941.

The Bletchley boffins working in that rusty tin-roofed Hut Three (it is still there) undoubtedly would have received the Germans' operational orders for the York raid. The problem was – could they have worked out York's code-number or operational code-name in time and have warned the city's authorities?

Some of the code-names for targets were well-known to the Intelligence, such as the numbers referring to Birmingham, Wolverhampton and Coventry. Even operational code-names were often easily guessed. Thus 'umbrella', which was associated with Chamberlain, famous for his gamp, who in his turn was associated with one specific town, could only mean 'Birmingham'. 'Unit price' was linked with Woolworth, where everything came in threepences and

THE HAND OF FRIENDSHIP. German ex-paratrooper Bernhard Carl Trautmann was a prisoner of war in the north, and went on to play for Manchester City. These pictures show him (left) being made welcome by his team mates, and (right) keeping goal at the Wembley Cup Final of 1955 (with his shoulder broken!)

sixpences, and Woolworth's was in due course identified as Wolverhampton, and so on . . .

Was the German operation order for the attack on York cracked in time? If it was, why wasn't York warned? And were there any sinister considerations behind that lack of warning?

Was the raid on York, which clearly had a strategic dimension (i.e. the knocking out of the railway system and crippling the supply of munitions to Russia), used to strengthen sagging home morale, turn world opinion against Germany, and justify what was coming next? We shall probably never know. All we do know is that one month and one day after York was bombed, Harris sent the first 1,000-odd RAF bombers (400 of them from Yorkshire fields) off to attack the Reich. They struck the ancient Rhenish cathedral city of Cologne with devastating force. 13,000 homes were destroyed in that raid, 6,000 badly damaged, 45,000 people rendered homeless and 5,000 citizens became casualties (469 killed).

It had been to no avail that the leader writer of the local Norwich paper stated after the city had suffered its second Baedeker raid, 'If Norwich Cathedral were destroyed, it would be no answer to bomb Cologne Cathedral'. The damage had been done. Total war had started with a vengeance! In Germany they commenced working on the new V-weapons, the V-1 and V-2, which would in due course devastate London and open up a new and terrible era in modern warfare. But that was to be in the future. In May 1942, Mr Churchill was signalling a triumphant Harris, after the Cologne raid: 'It is a herald of what Germany will receive, city by city, from now on.'

* * *

Now it was time to honour the dead.

Three thousand people attended the memorial service in the undamaged Minster one week later. The Press reported at the time, 'there were many tear-dimmed eyes among the congregation', when the Dean, the Very Rev. Milner White, who had won the D.S.O. himself in World War One, began his address.

He told that vast assembly: 'On that moonlit morning, dawning red before dawn was due, York paid its toll in the defence of our England, our liberty, our race. We do not grudge it. We have not complained. We will be proud of it. We mourn our dead and those whose homes were destroyed. We grieve over our ancient buildings which were our city's glory. We ache for the injured in hospital'.

'One day,' the Dean continued, looking around the congregation, 'we shall raise a memorial over our dead, for God forbid that they would be forgotten. It will be a new sort of memorial. We are used to records of sailors and soldiers ... These were the aged – so the inscription might run "who died for the children they would never see; these the fathers and mothers, who saved and hallowed England's homes under the ruins of their own; these the children who gave their years and lovely promise that freedom might play in our streets."'

'We remember you, our dead. God give you rest and light and joy and life – and York do them honour, who paid our toll with their all.'

Moving words! But that memorial to the dead of York's Longest Night, which the Dean had promised that bright May morning in 1942, was never erected. Three years later when it was all over, it was clear that the character of the nation was changing. Total war had had its effect. Most of the men and women who had fought the war in factory and at the front did not want, as the Dean had hoped that morning, to go back into 'the front line of the world battle'.

Something vital had been eroded in the intervening years. Neither the past nor the future interested them very much. Mostly they seemed just to want to go on living, getting on with the day-to-day business of simply existing. No one was interested in that April night when the dead children 'gave their years and lovely promise'.

Today, over 63 years later, that grim and bloody episode in York's long history is forgotten, save by those who took part in it, their number steadily growing smaller and smaller as the years go by. Perhaps it is best thus. Each summer those streets set ablaze by German bombers are crammed with admiring German tourists, half of them not even alive when it happened. Those schools which were damaged or destroyed by the bombs had long been sending the children – and grandchildren – of the citizens who went through the 'Baedeker' to York's twin town in Germany, Münster. It, too, is a cathedral city, but one which suffered

infinitely more damage by bombing than its twin did. Twenty years after the raid, Münster made its first financial contribution to the restoration of Coney Street. Forty years later, it was still helping generously when the city's pride, the Minster, was set ablaze, something which hadn't happened in 1942. Today, Britain and Germany understand each other better than at any other time this century. Today, German tourists fit into the city's tourist picture just as much as Americans, Canadians and half a score of other nationalities do. It is better so.

Back in May 1942 when the war was at its blackest and the British 8th Army was still on the run in Africa and Asia, with our American allies suffering defeat after defeat in the Pacific, it was proposed that the clock outside St. Martin-le-Grand church, which had stopped at 3.45 a.m. that terrible morning, should be kept at that time for ever, as a permanent memorial to the raid. In the heat and confusion of the war, the proposal was forgotten. Now that great old clock has been ticking away happily for 60-odd years or more. In a way that clock perched above a street, packed with tourists from all of the five continents for much of the year, is a symbol too – that on York's longest night, time didn't stop after all...

BOMBED – THIRTY YEARS LATER!

Mr. Bentley (Left) of Roseville Farm, Full Sutton, escaped unhurt when bombs fell around his farm that April in 1942. But he was not to get away completely untouched. Thirty years later, while he and his son were ploughing the land alongside the runway (below), the blade of the plough touched an old Mills bomb grenade. The explosion sent shrapnel through the tractor cab and took off part of his son's ear. Mr. Bentley well remembers how the crippled bombers would limp home in the morning from a night raid over Germany. In one week alone, four Halifax bombers crashed at the edge of the airfield – so near yet so far.

One German bomber was brought down in the raid. This was the work of Pilot Officer Yves Mahé of the Free French Air Force. A memorial to men of the Free French Air Force who lost their lives on subsequent raids over Germany now stands on the roadside outside the airfield at Elvington, near York, which is the site of the Yorkshire Air Museum and Allied Forces Memorial.

Halifax bombers of Number 4 Group operated from Elvington from October 1942 until the end of the war. Although the Free French Air Force squadrons left for France in October 1945, there were many of their personnel who stayed behind, married to wives they had met in York. (Below) the memorial, the old buildings on the airfield.

Gone Away

RAF Full Sutton – the last of the Wartime Bomber Stations.
Unmarked, unwanted, why?

Aircrew sleeping quarters.

Mess building
and air-raid shelter.

Below: Leo Kessler, well-known fiction writer, at former Bomber Command Station, RAF Full Sutton.

Neglected, overgrown and forgotten, most of the 90 airfields built in Yorkshire through two world wars lie in this dead and decaying condition. It is surely symbolic of the way Bomber Command was treated once the war in Europe was over. Though 56,000 aircrew died in carrying the war to Europe, they were never awarded their own campaign medal. The airfields, however, are still there, peopled by ghosts and visited occasionally by white-haired men.

The same story of neglect at RAF Marston Moor, Tockwith, once the station of Group Captain Leonard Cheshire V.C., D.S.O., D.F.C.

To the memory of William Milner

In 1984, a plaque was placed on the new wall of Platform 8a, in memory of Station Foreman William Milner, who entered a blazing building to reach urgently needed medical supplies, and was still holding the box when his body was later found. He was posthumously awarded the King's Commendation for Gallantry.

(Below) York station after extensive rebuilding in 1985.

Services back to normal – after 35 years

The first baptism in the church of St. Martin-le-Grand after the raid of 1942 took place on Sunday, 10th September 1978. The baby son of Mr. And Mrs. Joseph Oliver of Clifton Without was christened Keith Jean-Marie, the latter name marking the French nationality of his mother. It was a fitting ceremony – the only German plane shot down in the raid fell to the guns of a French pilot flying from Elvington near York.